To Sharon

with gratitude for your
great support and friendship

Nancy
Christmas 2005

ISBN:1 86476 196 2

AXIOM
AUSTRALIA

www.axiompublishers.com.au

Printed in Thailand

Timeless passages

Letterforms by Jim Billingsley
Illustrations by Lorraine Gum

All things in this creation exist within you,
and all things in you exist in creation;
there is no border between you and the closest thing,
and there is no distance between you and the farthest things,
and all things, from the lowest to the loftiest,
from the smallest to the greatest, are within you as equal things.
In one atom are found all the elements of the earth;
in one motion of the mind are found the motions
of all the laws of existence;
in one drop of water is found the secrets of all endless oceans;
in one aspect of you are found all the aspects of existence.

Kahlil Gibran

e good to yourself

Be yourself — truthfully.
Accept yourself — gratefully.
Value yourself — joyfully.
Forgive yourself — completely.
Treat yourself — generously.
Balance yourself — harmoniously
Bless yourself — abundantly.
Trust yourself — confidently.
Love yourself — wholeheartedly.
Empower yourself — confidently.
Give yourself — enthusiastically
Empress yourself — radiantly.

If I had my life to live again,
I'd try to make more mistakes next time.
I would relax; I would limber up;
I would be sillier than I have been on this trip.
I know of very few things I would take seriously.
I would take more trips. I would be crazier.
I would climb more mountains, swim more rivers,
and watch more sunsets...

If I had life to live over I would start barefoot earlier in the spring
and stay later in the fall. I would play hooky more.
I wouldn't make such good grades, except by accident.
I would ride on merry-go-rounds.
I'd pick more daisies.

Nadine Stair

esiderata

Go placidly amid the noise and haste, and remember
what peace there may be in silence. As far as possible
without surrender be on good terms with all persons.
Speak your truth quietly and clearly; and listen to others,
even the dull and ignorant; they too have their story.

Avoid loud and aggressive persons; they are
vexatious to the spirit. If you compare yourself with others,
you may become vain or bitter; for always there
will be greater and lesser persons than yourself.

Enjoy your achievements as well as your plans.
Keep interested in your own career, however humble;
it is a real possession in the changing of fortunes of time.
Exercise caution in your business affairs; for the
world is full of trickery. But let this not blind you to
what virtue there is; many persons strive for high ideals;
and everywhere life is full of heroism.

Be yourself. Especially, do not feign affection.
Neither be cynical about love; for in the face of all
aridity and disenchantment it is as perennial as the grass.

Take kindly the counsel of the years, gracefully surrendering
the things of youth. Nurture strength of spirit to shield you
in sudden misfortune. But do not distress yourself with imaginings.
Many fears are born of fatigue and loneliness.
Beyond a wholesome discipline, be gentle with yourself.

You are a child of the universe, no less than the
trees and the stars; you have a right to be here.
And whether not it is clear to you,
no doubt the universe is unfolding as it should.

Therefore be at peace with God, whatever you conceive
Him to be, and whatever your labours and aspirations
in the noisy confusion of life keep peace with your soul.

With all it's sham, drudgery, and broken dreams, it is
still a beautiful world. Be cheerful. Strive to be happy.

Easy to get depressed these days,
easy to feel afraid,
easy to think the world's gone mad,
easy for dreams to fade.
But the news we hear of the things we fear
should never blind us to
the many kind and splendid things
so many people do.

Far better it is to dare mighty things
To win glorious triumphs even though checkered by failure,
Than to take rank with those poor spirits
Who neither enjoy much nor suffer much
Because they live in the grey twilight
That knows neither victory nor defeat.

Theodore Roosevelt

There once was a man so despondent, his spirit was so torn up by cares and worry, that he decided to end it all. He started to walk across the city to a bridge, from which he planned to jump to a certain fate. However, as he walked, he made another critical decision. He said to himself, "If, on the way, I should meet someone with a friendly disposition, someone whose manner would bring a ray of hope into my life, I will turn back".

End of story

We don't know whether the troubled man jumped or not. If, while walking toward the bridge in a cloud of despair, that man had met you, what would he have met—a ray of hope, or ...?

Mother's Wrinkled Hands

Such beautiful, beautiful hands!
Though heart were weary and sad
Those patient hands kept toiling on
That her children might be glad.
I almost weep when looking back
To childhood's distant day!
I think how these hands rested not
When mine were at their play.

If there be righteousness in the heart,
There will be beauty in the character.
If there is beauty in the character,
There will be harmony in the home,
If there is harmony in the home,
There will be order in the nation.
If there is order in the nation,
There will be peace in the world.

Lao Tse

The difference between what we do
and what we are capable of doing
would suffice to solve most of the world's problems.

Mohandas K. Gandhi

When one door of happiness closes, another opens;
but often we look so long at the closed door
that we do not see the one which has been opened for us.

Helen Keller

I want to beg you,
as much as I can, to be patient
toward all that is unsolved in your heart
and to try to love the questions themselves
like locked rooms and like books
that are written in a very foreign tongue.
Do not seek the answers,
which cannot be given you
because you would not be able to live them.
And the point is to live everything.
Live the questions now.
Perhaps you will then gradually,
without noticing it,
live along some distant day into the answer.

Rainer Maria Rilke

ootprints

One night a man had a dream.
He dreamed he was walking along the beach with the Lord.
Across the sky flashed scenes from his life.
For each scene, he noticed two sets of footprints in the sand:
one belonging to him, and the other to the Lord.

When the last scene of his life flashed before him,
he looked back at the footprints in the sand.
He noticed that many times along the path of his life
there was only one set of footprints.
He also noticed that it happened at the very lowest
and saddest times in his life.

This really bothered him and he questioned the Lord about it.

"Lord, You said that once I decided to follow You,
You'd walk with me all the way. But I have noticed
that during the most troublesome times in my life,
there is only one set of footprints.
I don't understand why when I needed You most
You would leave me."

The Lord replied, "My son, My precious child,
I love you and would never leave you.
During your times of trial and suffering,
when you see only one set of footprints,
it was then that I carried you."

f today

If you planted hope today
In any hopeless heart.
If someone's burden was lighter
Because you did your part.
If you caused a laugh
That chased some tears away.
If tonight your name is named
When someone kneels to pray.
Then — your day
Has been well spent.

The deepest fear is not that we are inadequate.
The deepest fear is that we are powerful beyond measure.
It is our light, not our darkness, that most frightens us.
We ask ourselves, who am I to be brilliant, gorgeous,
talented and fabulous?
Actually, who are you not to be?
You are a child of God.
Your playing small does not serve the world.
There is nothing enlightened about shrinking
so that other people won't feel insecure about you.
We were born to manifest the glory of God that is within us.
It's not just in some of us; it's in everyone.
And as we let our own light shine,
we unconsciously give other people permission to do the same.
As we are liberated from our own fear,
our presence automatically liberates others.

Marianne Williamson

To everything there is a season,
And a time to every purpose under heaven:
A time to be born, and a time to die;
A time to plant, and a time to reap;
A time to keep, and a time to throw away;
A time to tear, and a time to mend;
A time to be silent, and a time to speak;
A time to love, and a time to hate;
A time for war, and a time for peace.

Ecclesiastes 3

Whatever mitigates the woes
or increases the happiness of others
— this is my criterion of goodness.
And whatever injures society at large,
or any individual, in it
— this is my measure of iniquity.

Robert Burns

f a child

If a child lives with hostility, he learns to fight.

If a child lives with criticism, he learns to condemn.

If a child lives with fear, he learns to be apprehensive.

If a child lives with jealousy, he learns to hate.

If a child lives with self-pity, he learns to be sorry for himself.

If a child lives with encouragement,
he learns self-confidence and integrity.

If a child lives with praise, he learns to be appreciative.

If a child lives with acceptance, he learns to love.

If a child lives with approval, he learns to like himself.

If a child lives with fairness, he learns justice.

If a child lives with honesty, he learns what truth is.

If a child lives with friendliness,
he learns that the world is a good place in which to live.

Fear is the main source of superstition, and one of the main sources of cruelty. To conquer fear is the beginning of wisdom.

Make new friends, but keep the old;
Those are silver, these are gold.
New-made friendships, like new wine,
Age will mellow and refine.
Friendships that have stood the test —
Time and change — are surely best.
Brow may wrinkle, hair grow grey;
Friendship never knows decay.
For 'mid old friends, tried and true,
Once more we our youth renew.

Joseph Parry

Why should we be in such desperate haste to succeed,
and in such desperate enterprises?
If a man does not keep pace with his companions,
perhaps it is because he hears a different drummer.
Let him step to the music which he hears,
however measured or far away.

Henry David Thoreau

The Power to Choose

At anytime, you can decide to alter the course of your life.
No one can ever take that away from you.
You can control your own destiny;
Make yourself do whatever is possible,
Make yourself become whatever you long to be.

You don't have to buy from anyone.
You don't have to work at a particular job.
You don't have to participate in any given relationship.
You can choose.
The choice is yours.
It is always your next move.

There is no greater illusion than fear,
no greater wrong than preparing to defend yourself,
no greater misfortune than having an enemy.

Whoever can see through all fear
will always be safe.

Lao-Tsu

Be courteous to all,
but intimate with few,
and let those few be well tried
before you give them your confidence.
True friendship is a plant of slow growth,
and must undergo and withstand
the shocks of adversity
before it is entitled to the appellãtion.

George Washington

Time is too slow for those who wait,
too swift for those who fear,
too long for those who grieve,
too short for those who rejoice.
But for those who love,
time is eternity.

Henry Van Dyke

To laugh often and much;
to win the respect of intelligent people
and the affection of children;
to earn the appreciation of honest critics
and endure the betrayal of false friends;
to appreciate beauty;
to find the best in others;
to leave the world a bit better,
whether by a healthy child,
a garden patch or a redeemed social condition;
to know even one life has breathed easier
because you have lived.
This is to have succeeded.

Ralph Waldo Emerson

If you think you are beaten, you are;
If you think you dare not, you don't;
If you like to win, but think you can't
It's almost a cinch you won't.

If you think you'll lose, you've lost;
For out in the world we find
Success begins with a fellow's will —
It's all in the state of mind.

If you think you are outclassed, you are;
You've got to think high to rise.
You've just got to be sure of yourself
Before you can win the prize.

Life's battles don't always go
To the stronger or faster man,
But sooner or later the man who wins
Is the one who thinks he can.

Ten Good Things

There are ten good things
for which no person has ever been sorry:
For doing good to all;
For speaking evil of no one;
For hearing before judging;
For thinking before speaking;
For holding an angry tongue;
For being kind to the distressed;
For asking pardon for all wrongs;
For being patient toward everybody;
For stopping the ear of a tale bearer;
For disbelieving most of the evil reports.

Life is without meaning.

You bring the meaning to it.
The meaning of life is
Whatever you ascribe it to be.
Being alive is the meaning.

o Know

You cannot bring prosperity by discouraging thrift.
You cannot help small men by tearing down big men.
You cannot strengthen the weak by weakening the strong.
You cannot lift the wage earner by pulling down the wage payer.
You cannot help the poor man by destroying the rich.
You cannot keep out of trouble by spending more than your income.
You cannot further brotherhood of men by inciting class hatred.
You cannot establish security on borrowed money.
You cannot build character and courage
by taking away man's initiative and independence.
You cannot help men permanently by doing for them
what they could and should do for themselves.

There is no easy walk to freedom anywhere,
and many of us will have to pass
through the valley of the shadow of death
again and again before we reach
the mountaintop of our desires.

Nelson Mandela

Life is a gift
Graciously given by mysteries unknown.
As all gifts, once received,
Our own attitude
Determines its true worth and value.
How shall you value your gift?

T. P. Carolat

he Time Is Now

If you are ever going to love me,
Love me now, while I can know
The sweet and tender feelings
Which from true affection flow.
Love me now
While I am living
Do not wait until I'm gone
And then have it chiselled in marble
Sweet words on ice-cold stone.
If you have tender thoughts of me,
Please tell me now.
If you wait until I am sleeping
Never to awaken,
There will be death between us,
And I won't hear you then.
So, if you love me even a little bit,
Let me know it while I am living,
So I can treasure it.

To awaken each morning with a smile
brightening my face, to greet the day with reverence,
to approach my work with a clean mind;
to hold ever before me,
even in the doing of little things,
the ultimate purpose toward which I am working;
to meet men and women with laughter
on my lips and love in my heart;
to be gentle, kind and courteous through all the hours;
to approach the night with weariness that ever woos sleep
and the joy that comes from work well done—
this is how I desire to waste wisely my days.

Thomas Dreier

Even a happy life
cannot be without a measure of darkness,
and the word happy would lose its meaning
if it were not balanced by sadness.
It is far better to take things as they come along
with patience and equanimity.

Carl Jung

Shrug off the restraints
that you have allowed others
to place upon you.
You are limitless.
There is nothing you
cannot achieve.
There is no sadness in life
That cannot be reversed.

If you are kind,
People may accuse you of selfish, ulterior motives;
Be kind anyway.

People are often unreasonable, illogical, and self-centred;
Forgive them anyway.

If you are successful, you will win some false friends
and some true enemies;
Succeed anyway.

If you are honest and frank, people may cheat you;
Be honest and frank anyway.

What you spend years building, someone could destroy overnight;
Build anyway.

If you find serenity and happiness, others may be jealous;
Be happy anyway.

The good you do today, people will often forget tomorrow;
Do good anyway.

Give the world the best you have, and it may never be enough;
Give the world the best you have anyway.

You see, in the final analysis, it is between you and God;
It was never between you and them anyway.

Mother Teresa

True happiness lies within you.
Waste no time and effort searching for peace
and contentment and joy in the world outside.
Remember that there is no happiness
in having or in getting, but only in giving.
Reach out.
Share.
Smile.
Hug.
Happiness is a perfume you cannot pour on others
without getting a few drops on yourself.

Og Mandino

I believe all suffering is caused by ignorance.
People inflict pain on others in the selfish pursuit
of their happiness or satisfaction.
Yet true happiness comes from a sense of peace and contentment,
which in turn must be achieved through the cultivation of altruism,
of love and compassion, and elimination of ignorance,
selfishness, and greed.

Dalai Lama

isten to the exhortation of the dawn!

Look to this day for it is life,
The very life of life!
In its brief course lie all the verities
And all the realities
Of your existence:
The bliss of growth,
The glory of action,
The splendour of beauty;
For yesterday is but a dream;
And tomorrow is only a vision;
But today well lived
Makes every yesterday
A dream of happiness and every tomorrow
A vision of hope.
Look well, therefore, to this day!
Such is the salutation of the dawn.

From the Sanskrit

What lies before us and what lies behind us
are small things compared to what lies within us.

Ralph Waldo Emerson

Cherish your visions; cherish your ideals;
cherish the music that stirs in your heart,
the beauty that forms in your mind,
the loveliness that drapes your purest thoughts,
for out of them will grow delightful conditions,
all heavenly environment;
of these if you but remain true to them,
your world will at last be built.

James Allen

orlds of fantasy

Humans, I believe, are naturally drawn to lives
and worlds outside of our own.
We revel in the existence of creatures
and even whole societies
beyond what we ourselves experience
in our everyday lives.
But have we gone so far
in creating worlds of fantasy
that we are missing the joy of other worlds
that already exist all around us?

David Suzuki

am not interested in picking up crumbs

I am not interested in picking up crumbs of compassion
thrown from the table of someone who considers himself my master.
I want the full menu of rights.

Bishop Desmond Tutu

Twenty years from now
you will be more disappointed
by the things that you didn't do
than by the ones you did do.
So throw off the bowlines.
Sail away from the safe harbour.
Catch the trade winds in your sails.
Explore… Dream… Discover.

Mark Twain

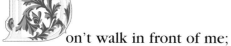on't walk in front of me;
I may not follow.
Don't walk behind me;
I may not lead.
Walk beside me and just be my friend.

Albert Camus

So live your life that the fear of death
can never enter your heart.
Trouble no one about their religion;
respect others in their view,
and demand that they respect your life.
Love your life, perfect your life,
beautify all things in your life.
Seek to make your life long
and its purpose to be
the service of your people.

Prepare a noble death song for the day
when you go over the great divide.
Always give a word or a sign of salute
when meeting or passing a friend,
or even a stranger, when in a lonely place.
Show respect to all people and bow to none.

When you arise in the morning
give thanks for the food
and for the joy of living.
If you see no reason for giving thanks,
the fault lies only in yourself.
Abuse no one and no living thing,
for abuse turns the wise ones to fools
and robs the spirit of its vision.

When it comes your time to die,
be not like those whose hearts
are filled with fear of death,
so that when their time comes
they weep and pray for a little more time
to live their lives over again in a different way.
Sing your death song and die
like a hero going home.

Tecumsh, Shawnee

have a dream

I say to you today, my friends, that in spite of the difficulties
and frustrations of the moment, I still have a dream.
It is a dream deeply rooted in the American dream.

I have a dream that one day this nation will rise up and live out
the true meaning of its creed: "We hold these truths to be self-evident:
that all men are created equal."

I have a dream that one day on the red hills of Georgia the sons of
former slaves and the sons of former slave-owners will be able to sit
down together at a table of brotherhood.

I have a dream that one day even the state of Mississippi,
a desert state, sweltering with the heat of injustice and oppression,
will be transformed into an oasis of freedom and justice.

I have a dream that my four children will one day live in a nation
where they will not be judged by the colour of their skin
but by the content of their character.

I have a dream today.

Martin Luther King

The secret of contentment is knowing how to enjoy what you have, and to be able to lose all desire for things beyond your reach.

Lin Yutang